Poetic Therapy

Poetic Therapy

POEMS & RHYMES TO HELP MANKIND

Greg Ware, M.A.

Copyrighted Material

Poetic Therapy

Copyright © 2017 by Twinapath Publishing. All Rights Reserved.

Library of Congress Cataloging-in-Publication data applied for.

No part of this publication may be reproduced, stored in a retrieval system or transmitted, in any form or by any means—electronic, mechanical, photocopying, recording or otherwise—without prior written permission from the publisher, except for the inclusion of brief quotations in a review.

For information about this title or to order other books and/or electronic media, contact the publisher:

Twinapath Publishing
justloveeverybody.com

ISBNs:
Print: 978-0-9968607-4-1
eBook: 978-0-9968607-5-8

Printed in the United States of America

Cover and Interior design: 1106 Design

An Ode to the human experience . . .

Table of Contents

CHAPTER 1 *Potpourri*

Father Time is Running out on Mother Nature 3

A Daughter's Prayer 4

My New Valentine 5

Didn't Pick My Parents 6

Mad at the Mirror 7

Secondhand Smoke 8

Athlete's Foot 10

Climate Change 11

It Takes 2 to Tango 12

Milk Bottles 13

Tree of Knowledge 14

Video Games 15

Fanimation 17

Remember 18

CHAPTER 2   *Colors of Love*

You're the Half, That Makes Me Whole 23

Send Me a Man. 24

Chasing Rainbows. 25

I Don't Care!. 26

The Internet. 27

A Good Man. 28

Happy Endings 29

My Fiancée 30

Beauty Mark 31

capital letters 32

My Everything 33

Monday thru Sunday. 34

My Name. 35

What's Wrong with Love? 36

Just to Get to Your Love 37

CHAPTER 3   *Laugh & Lust*

Bonnie and Clyde 41

The Urge to Merge 42

A Conversation Piece 43

Birth Control 44

Table of Contents

Hole in My Soul 45

Another Beer 46

Fairy Godmother 47

Pandora's Box 48

Hungry for Love 49

Nutty in My Fruitcake 50

This Ain't Love 51

Nuthin' I'd Rather Do 52

In the Mood 53

Someone, Somewhere, Somehow 54

Naked 55

My Cherry Mustang 56

My Way, or the Highway 57

CHAPTER 4 *Hot & Heavy*

Whale of a Tale 61

In It 4 a Minute 62

I Blow Clarinet 63

She's Ready 64

Chernobyl 65

She's Catching Feelings 66

Love Is Calling 67

C.O.D. 68

Love & Lust 69

Twice. 70

First Come, First Serve 71

A Conversation with My Cat 72

CHAPTER 5 *Life & Death*

Superstitions 75

Last Breath 76

If There Is a God 77

God Ain't on Facebook 78

God's Will 79

The Time Has Come 80

Call of Duty 81

A Terrorist Is Born 82

ANY IS TOO MANY! 83

Just Love Everybody 84

My Time to Shine! 85

Poetic Therapy 86

Acknowledgements 87

Meet the Author 89

ONE

Potpourri

Father Time is Running out on Mother Nature

"What happens when nature calls and there's no answer . . ."

The symptoms have been apparent for dozens of years.
A grim diagnosis, for both hemispheres.
To bury your head in the sand for an issue this wide-ranging.
While the polar caps are melting, and the temperature is changing.

The planet has a fever and most scientists agree.
That carbon is the cause, and it's our responsibility.
To change the ways, we pollute the land, air, and sea.
While preachy politicians lie to their constituencies.

Father Time doesn't care if we don't accept the facts.
He's perfectly fine with a brand new almanac.
Mother Nature's depressed and just took her last Prozac.
Corporate greed has her so angry, she's about to blow her stack!

So this is the last plea, to a tone deaf Legislature.
Father Time is indeed running out on Mother Nature . . .

A Daughter's Prayer

Girls be happy in your own skin,
and don't worry about opinions,
from boys who want to be men.

Realize that you're only human,
and it's better to imagine,
than follow every fashion.

So please remember,
when you have to struggle,
it could always be worse . . .

And never forget,
that life's a puzzle,
but you don't have to finish first!

Just celebrate the life you're livin',
with all your heart and soul.
Celebrate what you've been givin',
and be thankful for tomorrow!

My New Valentine

When our eyes first met and the world stopped spinning.
We realized that this was just the beginning,
of a relationship about to bloom.
Whoever thought that I'd be a groom?

When our lips kissed and I felt that tingle.
I knew right then and there I was no longer single,
because an angel had just captured my soul.
From that moment on, it was your household.

Sometimes love can seem like a game of Russian roulette.
But I feel like the Last Man Standing on the Bachelorette.
It's the grand finale, the definitive episode.
I caught the Leprechaun at the end of the rainbow.

My pot of gold is a lifetime with you,
as I'm filled with nothing but gratitude.
Is this a miracle or perhaps something divine?
Because it feels like heaven with my new Valentine . . .

Didn't Pick My Parents

I really don't agree,
but the date says Capricorn.
Yet who gets to select,
the day that they are born?

I've never understood,
how I got a name like Clarence.
Somethings you just can't leave,
up to your parents.

If it were my decision,
I'd prefer to live in Rome.
But I didn't get the chance to choose,
the place that I'd call home.

Who knew I had a hard time,
getting along with others?
When on the first day I got introduced,
to a sister and a brother.

I would go on but what's the point,
could I be any more coherent?
I chose a lot of things in life,
but I didn't pick my parents!

Mad at the Mirror

I was born with pale skin,
now riddled with pimples.
The punch line was crooked teeth,
when I was dreaming of dimples.

I've got a club foot,
and walk with a limp.
My nickname in grade school,
was Bubbles the Chimp.

I just look at food and gain a couple of pounds.
If eating were a race, I'd win The Triple Crown!
I get tired of all the daily criticism…
How do I speed up my metabolism?

My doctor informed me, I'm allergic to exercise.
So, I ate another slice of humble pie.
I watch TV and sometimes fantasize,
that I'll emerge from this cocoon a beautiful butterfly.

When I approach a pretty girl,
she doesn't want me near her.
Every day I wake up,
and I'm mad at the mirror!

Secondhand Smoke

I make my Penny the Hardaway,
and Billie is my only Holiday.
Every week I dream of being a V.I.P.
but I can't afford a ticket to the lottery.

I go to work in the morning,
cause bills gotta get paid.
I've got champagne tastes,
but still sipping Kool-Aid.
Try to keep a lil' savings,
for a rainy day.
But I'm drownin' in debt,
where's The Little Mermaid?

It seems the more I try to get ahead,
the farther behind I fall.
Keeping food on the table,
is a minor miracle.
My lover wants to move out of this
hole in the wall,
and my therapist's name,
is alcohol.

There's not enough makeup,
to fix my credit line.
If money were good looks,
then call me Frankenstein.
I'll tell you what I'm about to buy,
to end this anecdote.
The only thing on sale today,
is secondhand smoke . . .

Athlete's Foot

Starry-eyed kids dream of being the next Michael Jordan.
Yet somehow end up bawling at the court with a warden.

While tiger moms coach their players to excel.
Because job openings are scarce in the NFL.

Many fathers brag about how Johnny can swing the bat.
However, he's having difficulty reading The Cat In The Hat . . .

They think they're raising the next great superstar.
But he's only half as tall as Abdul-Jabbar.

Great Expectations that usually fall apart.
When he should have been studying, but was at the ballpark.

I know you didn't ask for my input.
But you're being delusional about your athlete's foot . . .

Climate Change

Is the planet changing,
or just coming apart at the seams?
If only the world was as simple and sweet,
as a dozen Krispy Kremes.

There are three sides to every issue,
and the truth is elusive at best.
I see racial trashing and immigrant bashing,
as I fly Over the Cuckoo's Nest.

Yes, the oceans are rising,
and justice is dying at an alarming rate.
Yet, who knew marriage would be defined,
right after Will and Grace . . .

It's hard to watch cable news,
as opinions are polarized.
Is there any sand left in the hourglass,
on The Days of Our Lives?

It Takes 2 to Tango

When you told me that my best friend,
was having your baby.
If looks could kill,
well you'd be pushing up daisies.

You've got a boat load of excuses,
while the conclusion is foregone.
It takes 2 to Tango,
do you have a leg to stand on?

You were my heart's hero,
our own Robin Hood.
Now I'm stuck out on a limb,
while you're lost in the woods.

A match made in heaven,
thought I'd caught a falling star.
Elvis has left the building,
so close, but no cigar!

Milk Bottles

Your wife just paid the doctor,
for two Magic Mountains.
She keeps trying to drink out of a youthful fountain.

You flew in like Captain Underpants,
about to save the planet.
But she's a Nasty Girl and her name's not Janet.

I'm great at dispensing advice,
so just call me Yoda.
It's time for you to sell that old Toyota.

If you want to keep up,
with God's new milk bottles.
Go buy a Little Red Corvette that you can throttle.

Then call up your doctor,
because this problem could be major.
He's got a pill to make you feel like a teenager!

Tree of Knowledge

You sit here crying,
with waves that seem tidal.
When you're more talented than an American Idol.

Just because he left you,
for another.
Girl, you better listen to your old grandmother.

You need someone educated,
or with a little ambition.
You'll never be secure with a broke musician.

Stability is the cornerstone,
of all relationships.
Don't you deserve somebody who can commit?

You need to pick your fruit,
from the Tree of Knowledge.
Stop hanging out in clubs, and go to college!

Video Games

"I put my X in the Box to accept the Call of Duty, to guard
   the PlayStation."

When I enter the World of Warcraft
everyone's shooting at each other.
I went Madden and killed Super Mario's Brother.

I never wore a Halo,
had a Need for Speed.
Call me Resident Evil with an Assassin's Creed!

I once was convicted of
Grand Theft Auto.
Got Half-Life for 3 Strikes and that's my motto.

Pac Man, G-Man
hell—I play the Game of Thrones.
My Final Fantasy is to be left alone.

You hunt for Pokemon,
while I Raid the Tomb.
I never have to get out of my Fruit of the Looms.

Somehow I fell in love
when I was visiting The Sims.
Wound up doing the Donkey Kong at the Holiday Inn.

I finally found some graphics
lit like Kurt Cobain.
But by next week they'll introduce a brand new video game.

Fanimation

My friends call me Homer cause I got a kid named Bart.
Who still cries every time they kill Kenny on South Park.

We're sitting here waiting on a pizza from a fellow named Fry.
My dog Brian keeps complaining, he's not a Family Guy.

Just got a text from Beavis who I think is brain-dead.
He's almost as smart as my neighbor, Butt-Head.

It says my pizza got stuck in a time machine.
Fry got jacked by some Titans who are barely Teens!

Who should I call—Spider, Super, or maybe Batman?
But Marge says they're trapped in fantasyland.

Then why are the Simpsons the King of the Hill once again?
Until Gravity Falls and we meet Jake and Finn.

This whole poem has been an Adventure in Time.
A tribute to the animated creativity of mankind . . .

Remember

Remember when they used
to play music on MTV?
Before they changed
the definition of reality.

Remember when the news
was for everyone?
Now there's a channel for your opinion.
Remember when elections
didn't remind you of Schindler's List.
Who knew that a President could be an Apprentice?

Remember when you went to court
and the Judge wasn't Judy?
Might as well crack open
another fortune cookie.
Remember when sports
weren't on 24 hours a day?
Mounting athletes on pedestals that don't elevate.

Remember when it was either
13 channels or the radio?
Now you can't get laid
without some HBO.
Remember when porn was on tape
and that fuzzy screen?
Today you don't even need a Playboy Magazine.

Remember when everyone
wasn't a talk show host?
Who gave Steve Harvey
a license to diagnose?
The moral of this story
should be clear as a bell.
This planet just down-loaded a ticket to hell . . .

TWO

Colors of Love

You're the Half, That Makes Me Whole

There's no one here watching football, and I hold the remote
Cook what I want for dinner, no more taking a vote
I don't have to diet, just to impress him
Yet I can't help but wonder, when will this end . . .

I've got the whole bed to myself, and I set the alarm
Maybe fall asleep naked, who's giving a darn
I don't wear much make-up, can I get an amen
Yet I can't but wonder, when will this end . . .

Every once in a while, I go down memory lane
Every now and then, I start to feel the pain
Of a heart that's empty, emotions out of control
You're the half, that makes me whole . . .

Send Me a Man

Lord knows I'm on my knees to pray,
but first there's something I gotta say.
I know for millennials things can be tough,
but I've been single for long enough.

I thank you for the clouds up in the sky,
yet here's a question, and I've got to know why.
You know I've been the best person I could possibly be,
now don't you have a man just right for me?

You gave us majestic mountains and skies so blue.
Well how about a guy that compares to You?

Send me a man, that's what I wish,
and this time don't make him so selfish.
Send me a man for the rest of my life,
one without all those stereotypes.
Send me a man who will commit,
and this time make him affectionate.

* * *

You want a man that doesn't exist,
got to build him from scratch and there's a waiting list . . .

Chasing Rainbows

Been so long since I left you,
and I'm still chasing rainbows.
Seems like I hear a love song,
every time the wind blows.

I sit at this bar with options wide open,
and my drinking goggles sure got me hopin.
Too many fish in my Long Island Ice Tea,
so it's hard not to have a fantasy . . .
Some people dream of Sex on the Beach,
yet what I want, is always out of my reach.

Love can have you walking on air,
while lust has left me in despair.
The perfect girl for me,
may be the one I had . . .

I Don't Care!

You've been sponging off me since the day we met,
now my credit's all bad and I'm rolling in debt.
I hear you're all over town, just spreadin' ya seed,
got a flower right here, and ya watering weeds.
Mickey take your Mouse and get out of my house!

* * *

I don't care, now that you're not here.
You couldn't leave any quicker?
You'll never see me shed a tear,
for you or your liquor . . .

With so many fish in the sea, I surf the Internet.
Gotta a Facebook Romeo, and I'm his Juliet.
A fairy-tale ending, just like Green Eggs and Ham,
now I'm tweeting and posting on Instagram.

Pictures of just the two of us,
riding on the Magic School Bus!
Everything is just coming up roses,
while your memory slowly decomposes . . .

The Internet

When ya walked into my life girl, I got a whole new outlook.
Babe found me while she was searching on Facebook.
Next thing that I know is she's knocking on my door.
And my heart opened up so wide, cause it needed a savior!

We sat and chatted all night long, like a couple of lovebirds.
You said I was the perfect host, and ya gave me your password.
We checked out YouTube's latest videos.
You let me plug right into to your port, and I had to
    download!

You can tweet or you can text,
this was much more than sex.
Perhaps I never would have found love,
without the Internet . . .

A Good Man

You say you've been used and abused, well you're not the first.
So just don't shut the door, because that would be worse.
Major mistakes have been made based on emotion.
Even Sleeping Beauty needed a magic potion . . .

You could live a thousand lifetimes,
and never figure out a man.
It seems like they don't grow up,
just like Peter Pan.

Yet every blue moon,
you can find a diamond in the dirt.
A ray of sunshine and some water,
perhaps you won't get hurt.

Good men don't come in bunches—They don't grow on trees.
A good man will last a lifetime—You've got to plant the right
    seeds.

Happy Endings

Like a thief in the night, you slipped into my life,
and put these stars up in my eyes.
You turned on the charm, someone ring the alarm,
your kiss gives me butterflies.

It could be breakfast in bed, or a restaurant instead,
you know how to improvise.
Treats me like a queen, not a puppet on a string,
your love could win a Nobel Prize.

Your voice is as sweet as honey.
Your touch feels better than money.
Your smile's so bright it's sunny.
You laugh and the world seems funny.

So love me tender while you're spreading my wings.
It feels like we're flying, love happy endings . . .

My Fiancée

I can't live without you,
and don't mind if the road's uphill.
Your worth so much more to me,
than any dollar bill.

Whenever you're not here,
baby this heart stands still.
My prescription says loneliness,
and you're the only pill.

You know I need you more,
than a wish on Christmas Day.
And I'm not the kind of guy,
to ever up and walk away.

If you have any doubts,
well you've seen my resume.
I got down on bended knee,
and now you're my fiancée . . .

Beauty Mark

As long as a soul needs a mate,
and my heart doesn't ache.
As long as water is wet,
and two's a duet.

As long as Winnie's the Pooh,
and Scooby can Doo.
As long as Snow remains White,
and football's on Monday Night.

As long as Sesame's a Street,
and in Miami there's Heat.
As long as Beverly has Hills,
and diets have pills.

As long as there's an "i" in phone,
and Fred's a Flintstone.
You'll always live in my heart,
as long as beauty leaves a mark . . .

capital letters

for YOUR LOVE i thirst,
every day IS like the FIRST.
now that i've reached manhood,
I NEED YOU more than i should.

for all that IT'S worth,
you're THE GREATEST show ON EARTH.
never misunderstood,
got a DOCTORate in FEELGOOD.

MY SOUL has never-ever,
had a better MATE.
AN ANGEL sent FROM HEAVEN,
just to keep MY HEART safe.

you're the LIGHT OF MY LIFE,
MY BETTER HALF.
the capital letters,
in each paragraph . . .

My Everything

You say you're ready for commitment,
and I know that you're sincere.
Yet most of my relationships,
only end in tears.

I hope this will be different,
in this land that love forgot.
I pray it isn't like the others,
a failure in Camelot.

When fate brought us together,
two spirits were united.
The souls of all who've gone before,
you're really not invited.

I'm at a point in my life,
where chivalry is king.
I hope that you're the maiden,
who becomes my everything . . .

Monday thru Sunday

Wishing nights were much longer,
when you hold me closely.
I only want to do,
what makes you happy.

The quality time that we spend alone,
makes up for when we're apart.
You wrote every day I love you more,
on my Hallmark greeting card.

From weekends to weekdays,
Winter, Spring, Summer, or Fall.
If it's on the calendar,
hear this once and for all.

Monday thru Sunday, are the days I'll be loving you.
Monday thru Sunday—Holidays too!

My Name

Some people are like a Rolling Stone,
missing a chromosome.
Then they end up all alone,
because their heart can't find a home.

Some people play The Dating Game,
instead of Singin' in the Rain.
It's a lowdown dirty shame,
to think that love's a ball and chain.

It's a joy I can't contain,
with so many trips down memory lane.
Let's all toast the champagne,
to the girl that I'm giving, my name!

What's Wrong with Love?

I'm falling too fast, cause I feel too much.
I only think about your tender touch.
Babe can't you see, through the angel dust?
Impossible to hide, it's so obvious . . .

There's a thing called love, and a thing called lust.
I left all the games at Toys R Us.
When it comes to my heart, it's serious.
Isn't this something, we should discuss?

What's wrong with love?
It could lead to a heartache.
Yet, that's a chance I'm willing to take.

What's wrong with love?
If it brings us together,
Like a Heatwave in Hades, Always and Forever.

Just to Get to Your Love

Been working all day, trying to turn water into wine.
Time seems to stand still, cause I can't get you out of my mind.

Memories invade my daydreams; we're cutting our wedding cake.
Loving you is so real, when I wake up my belly aches.

I hope that you're ready, when love opens the door.
Kissing the sweet lips, that I mount on Rushmore.

If the world is a jungle, then you're my Lion King.
I hear a symphony, when you pull my heartstrings.

There's no place I'd rather be, than sharing your company.
I'll take a bus, a train, the subway, or a plane—Just to get to your love!

THREE

Laugh & Lust

Bonnie and Clyde

For love's sake, I got rehabilitated.
My cellmate, is inebriated.
Those heartaches, were premeditated.
Incarcerate? No, I've been vindicated.

I may not be your first love,
but I'm going to be your last.
Whenever we're together,
I've escaped from Alcatraz.

There's a part of me, only you set free,
saving us years of therapy.
The evidence proves an innocent man is hard to find,
because the sentence is more than a lifetime.

We all carry some shackles,
as emotions sometimes collide.
I plead guilty of love in the first-degree,
just like Bonnie and Clyde.

The Urge to Merge

I'm not the best driver, my eyes wander a bit.
I even got a ticket watching Sunset Strip.

Can't stay in my lane, and refuse to carpool.
And today I fell in love at Traffic School.

We went on a test drive, to open her up wide.
She whispered, "Like going commando, I'm not sanctified."

When I hit the brakes, she just stepped on the gas.
Is there any better way to get whiplash?

Then the light turned green, and the coast was clear.
Now her head's bouncing in my rear view mirror.

When she felt—my seat belt, I heard her say,
"I feel the urge to merge on this freeway . . ."

A Conversation Piece

It started off so innocent,
with just the bat of an eye.
Had nothing to do with home,
where I was always satisfied.

Should I blame human nature,
or the curse of being a man?
I never imagined I would be,
on the witness stand.

After the first time Your Honor,
yes—I wanted it to end.
Yet no matter how hard I tried,
it happened again and again.

I've never been so embarrassed,
to be caught by the police.
In the back seat of our mini-van,
with my conversation piece!

Birth Control

When we met you said you'd give me the world,
and in this galaxy—I'm Supergirl.
You had a millennium to sow your wildest oats,
and you were all done chasing petticoats.

I took you in when you lost your job,
even gave you a key to the door knob.
Letcha sleep in late while I flew to work,
and now I realize you're not my Captain Kirk . . .

We were so happy, living on cloud nine.
But then I heard it through the spacevine,
you're having Close Encounters with the Wrong Kind.
Load up your Ford Explorer, and leave the moonshine!

You broke my heart and crushed my soul,
as our romance zoomed past the threshold.
You blew up something so beautiful,
I wish your mom had used Birth Control . . .

Hole in My Soul

Things have never been the same,
since the day you departed.
It was over just about as fast as it started.
From love at first sight,
a match like no other.
It almost felt like a sister or brother.

I gave you enough rope,
to hang more than yourself.
All that seemed to do, was make your heart melt.
We grew closer and closer,
and could have been twins.
An enchanting love story, without the fairy tale end.

No more nightmares about duels,
or the constant hassle.
Tell me, why did you decide to return to his castle?
Now I'm killing my sorrow,
with shots of Cuervo Gold.
I hope these spirits fill up, this hole in my soul . . .

Another Beer

They say that absence,
makes the heart grow fonder.
I think about us and it makes me wonder.

That's a heavy spell,
you've got me under.
Because no one's been able to steal your thunder.

Sometimes I reminisce,
about when our souls first kissed.
I never imagined that I could take,
your kindness for weakness?

Then you found that lingerie,
and I wished my life had instant replay.
Now just like Casper, you've disappeared.
I think I'll have another beer . . .

Fairy Godmother

We met at the club, and just like a drug,
got hooked on one another.

I had no defense, for compliments,
after shots of Christian Brothers.

Your kisses were so passionate,
that I almost felt smothered.

It made no sense, to be this intense,
so I asked my Fairy Godmother.

* * *

She said—"He'll spare no expense, but this is nonsense,
he really wants your brother!"

Pandora's Box

Hangin out at the party, I met a girl named Pandora.
Spent the rest of the night trying to open her box.

She had a twin sister, whose name was Laura,
They were both 'just right' with Goldilocks.

I walked them to their car, trying to get at least one number.
Was I barking up the wrong tree?

They kept playing games, like Dumb and Dumber.
Until their husbands showed up angry.

Needless to say, there was quite a scuffle.
How do you stop a nosebleed?

I need a good luck charm, having nothing but trouble.
So I just bought Bugs Bunny's feet!

Hungry for Love

The love I want is overdue.
It's time for us to rendezvous.
This fried chicken is in the nude,
and now I'm starving for more than food.

I like my meat nice and tender,
seasoned with unconditional surrender.
Just like breakfast, lunch, or dinner.
I miss your love, and I get thinner.

I'm going to need more than one bite,
to satisfy my appetite.
Will I swallow, you bet your life.
I'm not counting calories tonight.

A full course of fun, not a Family Feud.
I'm hungry for love, and thirsty for you.

Nutty in My Fruitcake

Make my bedrock while ya touching my soul.
Bake me slowly like a casserole.
I might be sitting on a pot of gold,
but you're scoring like it's the Rose Bowl.

When you make love to me—There's nothing left to debate
When you make love to me—You're Superman with no cape
When you make love to me—The world moves—my earth
    quakes
When you make love to me—I'm soggy as Cornflakes.

When you make love to me—It feels like I'm jailbait
When you make love to me—I never plan to escape
When you make love to me—From late night till daybreak
When you make love to me—Go nutty in my Fruitcake.

This Ain't Love

Like an angel you were heaven sent,
and loving me was the first Commandment.
We stay in all weekend and you never complain,
just being with me and you're entertained.

I go to work and can't concentrate . . .
Spend all day dreaming about the love we make.
I'm a Superhero, who can't feel any pain.
But without you baby, I'm just Bruce Wayne.

This ain't love, it's something stronger.
This ain't love, it lasts much longer.
This ain't love, and I'm not trying to be clever.
But it can't be love, because it's forever!

Nuthin' I'd Rather Do

I enjoy going to the movies and eating popcorn,
or grooving to a jazz man blowing his horn.
I like having friends over to watch football,
and having way too much cholesterol.

It's fun going to parties and dancing real close,
or sitting in a hot tub double-dipping Fritos.
I love taking you shopping for sheer lingerie,
or surprising you with flowers on no special day.

I enjoy giving massages while we lie in the sand,
or spending the whole day at Disneyland.
I like whispering sweet nothings to you late at night,
and pretending it matters who wins pillow fights.

Yet there's nuthin' in the world that I'd rather do,
than make sweet love to you . . .

In the Mood

When I get in the mood,
wanna be in the nude.
So baby put your lips on mine.

I'm hot and so are you,
just like some soul food.
Good love is so hard to find.

Somethin I gotta say,
wanna go all the way.
My Streetcar is Named Desire.

I'll be ya protégé,
so if we're gonna play.
Plug on in this amplifier.

My arms are open, ya got me hopin'.
We can make this more than a weekend.
Ring around the Rosie, it's time to get cozy.
Where'd you hide the mandolin?

Someone, Somewhere, Somehow

When I metcha baby, everything just clicked.
You loved everything about me from toenails to lipstick.
That's why I wanna give you my body and soul,
to have and to hold.
Because everything aboutcha is so wonderful.

Now that I'm your lady, well I need a list.
Write down everything that you desire, and seal it with a kiss.
There's nothing in the world that I won't do, sell my Subaru,
and move to Honolulu.
Let somebody else sing the blues!

Someone, Somewhere, Somehow . . .
There's somebody for me—it's you!

Naked

Let's get naked so I can take it.
Smoke it like Cheech and Chong.
Let's get naked so I can shake it.
Sounds like our new theme song.

We met at the club,
a couple of weeks ago.
I bought you a drink,
and took an arrow.

Cupid don't miss,
when the stars are aligned.
Now my heart's in heaven,
dressed in Anne Klein.

Mother Nature has spoken,
and she says I'm your girl.
The odds are in our favor,
it's you and me against the world.

My Cherry Mustang!

Before you take me out on a test spin.
I need to see your license, cause I'm about to sin.
You better kick the tires and check under the hood.
You gonna make my day, like Clint Eastwood.

Gotta slide your key on in, and bend it to the right.
Let me warm up for a minute, it feels a little tight.
I'll grab the stick shift, and make it straighten up.
Just drop it in first, then whip this cream puff.

Watch out for all the curves on the wet road ahead.
You better hold on tight, cause I'm a thoroughbred.
Slowly dip at the hip, and slip it into overdrive.
If you go flat on the first lap, use the Jaws of Life.

Pay no attention to the odometer, those are freeway miles.
What did you expect, I'm not a juvenile.
In this car-pool lane, you can drive drunk.
I'll even let you drop a load in the trunk.

So pull up to my bumper, and give it your everythang.
You're gonna love riding in my Cherry Mustang!

My Way, or the Highway

On weekends, you go out with your girlfriends,
leaving me at home—baby all alone.
Yet even when you're here,
I gotta share you with Facebook, Twitter, and all those
    games.
Too much technology, no apology,
Babe, that's just how my heart feels . . .

Can't pretend, you know I'm only human,
down to the bone—full of testosterone.
Yet even when I'm here,
you're calling Sherry and Mary, and texting what's her name.
Too much technology, no apology,
Babe, you're asleep at the wheel.

I need to be as important as foreplay,
between a pigeon and a blue jay.
And this might sound a little cliché.
But it's my way, or the highway . . .

FOUR

Hot & Heavy

Whale of a Tale

If size doesn't matter,
then call me Moby Dick.
It's the motion of the ocean,
that sinks most ships.

I like the calm before the storm,
so we float for a while.
Then you unfurl your sails,
and I launch my missile.

It's a direct hit,
as it pierces the hull.
A tidal wave of emotions crest,
when things get physical.

I try my best to ride the surf,
until we both reach land.
But that's a whale of a tale,
I hope you understand . . .

In It 4 a Minute

You came at me like you wuz hard,
ran everything on the boulevard.
Never down on ya chips—always flossin',
I letcha hit the skins—letcha toss-em.

Now I find out you were only perpetrating.
You said you wuz the bomb when it came to lovemaking.
Then boom! You blew up, just a little too quick.
But at least this problem can be licked.

When I make love—it's by the hour.
Bon Appetit—it's never sour.
Keeping it sweet—just like a flower.
My Cream of Wheat—you will devour.

A "G" is supposed to last long, be strong,
and tell me when I do wrong.
Don't be so quick with the trigger!
I thought it was bigger?
You wuz in it, for a minute . . .

I Blow Clarinet

Once in a while I surf the Internet,
and today I found a smile, sweeter than chocolate.
She sent me a Snapchat of her silhouette,
and said her sex tape's available on cassette.

We met for dinner just after sunset,
and ordered the soup with the alphabet.
Bought some drinks while we hung out at the bar,
and she's fascinated because I play guitar.

My fingers raise the pitch like a Capo on her neck.
She starts strumming my thigh, and it's a duet.
I'm plucking the strings next to her asset.
While she sings in my ear,
I blow clarinet . . .

She's Ready

Uh-oh, there's a camel toe, and the monkey's out the cage.
A see-thru thong, it won't be long, before we misbehave.
First let's cop a buzz, we'll start with some champagne.
Cristal, Screwball, more alcohol, and then I'll make it rain.

We make it back to my place, after painting the whole town red.
With all that butter baby, I know you're gonna spread.
You seemed so fascinated on my friend with the one eye.
The next thing I know you're swallowing, much more than
    your pride.

You could have written a book on love,
because you're great between the covers.
But you're just not the kind of girl,
that I'd take home to mother.

I had a ball twisting you up,
like a string of spaghetti.
And if there were only two words in the universe,
they would be—She's Ready.

Chernobyl

My new man is full of passion.
Got a PhD in unzip and unfasten.
I'm at an age where lust is in fashion.
But I almost got killed by a booty assassin.

We met at a concert for Billy Joel.
He was dressed in black Kenneth Cole.
Told me I resembled a centerfold.
How could I know he was on parole?

Took me to my favorite watering hole.
Dipped his finger in my sugar bowl.
It was hotter than a manifold.
Next thing I knew, I felt my Tootsie Roll.

He knocked his balls threw my field goal.
I rode him like a stripper's pole.
Pushed me way past loves threshold.
Then I exploded like Chernobyl!

She's Catching Feelings

She's catching feelings, got her walking on ceilings.
Wants to be my Boo, but what's a playa to do?
Cause now I'm catching them, oh now I'm catching them
    too . . .

Was going to smash and dash, but once I cut the pie.
It felt so good I had another slice, and spent the night.
Got an ass I could not pass, like pastrami on rye.
Didn't even drink nuthin', yet feelin so high!

I usually mash for cash, til they're satisfied.
Lie about how much I care, and then backslide.
However, this seems different, and I don't know why.
Didn't even smoke nuthin', but I'm touchin the sky!

Lord knows I gave you the business, until we were just about
    senseless.
On Sunday, let's get down on our knees and pray for
    forgiveness!

Love Is Calling

We should have been a couple a long time ago.
But I was with her, and you were with him.
Bumped into you at the pharmacy,
and that's how our story begins.

Your kids are grown and mine live in Buffalo,
so we're not going out on a limb.
Both past our prime and twice divorced,
remember we're only human.

Serendipity brought us together,
yet destiny is never random.
And feelings seldom change,
they're only abandoned.

At our age my dear, there's no more time for stalling.
Need an answer to your prayers, well—love is calling . . .

C.O.D.

I'm sending you my heart C.O.D.,
and hope you respond A.S.A.P.
I'm in this for eternity,
and it's always polite to R.S.V.P.

I believe that fairy tales,
can sometimes come true.
So I'm mailing you a package,
that should arrive soon.

When you open up my emotions,
please handle them with care.
If dropped or somehow damaged,
love's in a wheelchair.

Just return them to sender,
if you're not completely certain.
Let's Make a Deal so you don't miss,
what's behind the curtain.

Love & Lust

Love wants ta whisper in ya ear
Lust wants ya thong for a souvenir
Love is grown by the seeds you plant
Lust is handcuffs and lubricant
Love is always worth waiting for
Lust wants to come in the back door
Love can happen at first sight
Lust wants to bang the neighbor's wife
Love wants massages and a back rub
Lust wants the twins in a hot tub

But remember . . .
From true love there is no escape
While lust can always masturbate!

Twice

The grass looks much greener, on the other side.
I see a lot more weeds on the other guys.
You wanna beat around the bush, or just mow the lawn.
Let's test your skills, deep down in the Amazon.

Take a bite of this apple, it's not a Capital offense.
You'll feel like Superman, not a flaccid Clark Kent.
Then I'll spoil you rotten, and letcha hit the Jackpot!
You know the 1st Prize is—I lick the lollipop.

* * *

You ate the whole damn thing, including the core.
Had me speaking in tongues and praising the Lord.
Now it's time to play swallow the leader,
so you can feel the kiss of paradise.
To show you all my moves,
we'll have to do it twice . . .

First Come, First Serve

They call me First Come—First Serve,
but I'm really just a bimbo.
Get in line—watch the curves,
place ya order at the window.

Get a couple of breasts,
a thigh and maybe some wings.
Don't forget about the legs,
you'll wanna spread dem thangs.

They come with our own sauce,
called the Sweet "G" Spot.
Just eat it all right here,
behind the parking lot.

You'll lick more than your fingers,
I come right off the grill.
These buns caress the meat,
and there's free refills.

So put your money on the counter,
and get ready for a meal.
We'll super-size it if ya mounter,
in your Oldsmobile.

A Conversation with My Cat

I went to the shelter and got a Siamese cat,
thought she might like a brand new habitat.
Had all of her shots and every vaccination,
so I took her home after a small donation.
Now she lies in my bed like she's on vacation,
leaving hairy balls on my pillow—no consideration.

I asked her just what her problem was,
and to my surprise, she said it was all because . . .

        * * *

There's a tomcat down the street, who keeps trying to mate.
I said let's wait, we haven't had one date!
You know I need a little conversation,
and he wants to start with penetration?
Then the Tabby next door has an education,
but I hear he got freaky with a gay Dalmatian.
He swears it was only masturbation,
but I think he's on the down low, and takes dictation.

        * * *

I told her that was quite a revelation,
but before there's any fornication.
She might want to ask for some compensation?
It costs money to feed another population.
Was this all just my imagination?
So I poured a stiff drink and prayed for salvation . . .

FIVE

Life & Death

Superstitions

It's Friday the 13th,
and I found a four-leaf clover.
Was it beginner's luck or is my life over.

So I crossed my fingers,
while knocking on wood.
Kept praying to make it out the hood.

They say bad luck always comes in threes,
and my address is 666.
But I got my lucky rabbit's foot,
and I wear a crucifix.

Tripped over a black cat,
and broke a couple of mirrors.
Yet, with these itchy palms my destiny couldn't be clearer.

Just wished upon a falling star,
and received a premonition . . .
Walk under a ladder anytime you like,
and give up superstitions!

Last Breath

You can take being unappreciated, like a teacher in school.
Or being upstaged, by a Beatle from Liverpool.

You can take overpaying, for a dirty lap dance.
Or a crabby patty, from Sponge Bob Square Pants.

You can take being ignored by a waiter in Rome,
while being stood up for dinner by Sharon Stone.

You can take being overcharged for sunglasses from Prada,
or paying through the nose for a Piña Colada.

You can take being hated because you have your own style.
When you're really just answering The Call of the Wild.

Everyone is dreading the darkness of death.
It really doesn't matter if you're an actor named Seth,
or a Queen like Elizabeth.

The one thing in life you never want to take,
is your last breath!

If There Is a God

When I come home from work, and turn on the news.
Then remember what gave me yesterday's blues.
Some people worship a Savior that's green,
and I'm so used to it, it's almost routine.

When I'm sleeping at night, I dream of a place.
Where everything's peaceful, there's only one race.
To encourage hate is much too time consumin'.
Why debate whether you're a man or a woman?

I wonder if the fellow Upstairs,
can hear me now in this prayer.

If there is a God, just give me a sign.
Not a wink or a nod, but something divine.
If there is a God, I wanna know.
We all need a path to follow . . .

God Ain't on Facebook

God don't follow you on Facebook, he's got bigger fish to fry.
He don't tweet, text, or Instagram—and here's the reason why.

He's got babies to deliver, all over the whole wide world,
and a long list of prayers—from every boy and girl.

He's gotta deal with all dem racists, knocking on the Pearly Gates.
They always seem surprised to find—they have a different fate.

He's got a place for politicians, who aren't concerned about the poor.
It seems they forgot to read the book, they say that they adore!

He's so busy up in heaven, there's not much time to spare.
Those angels love to party—and always want Him there.

The egos of some people, do you really think He cares?
About any and everything you Like, post, or share!

God's Will

If God is truly omnipotent and in total control.
Then everyone on earth has an Immortal soul.
So, you thanked him for the first black President.
It was not only a miracle, but heaven-sent.

Well now another election has passed.
Where are the faithful and steadfast?
If God is in charge of supervision.
Then why do you question his decisions?

I have a list of things that he could explain.
Like Hitler, hatred, and hurricanes.
When genetics can decide sexual orientation.
Why would the Lord create an abomination?

So, if you wonder why God neglected Hillary and Bill.
Well maybe he died a while ago, and didn't leave a Will.

The Time Has Come

Gangbangers go back to school,
and learn to stop saggin', let knowledge rule.
Those good ole boys, ya got way too many toys.
Take the hoods off hate, don't eat the Devil's food cake.

Corporations, too big to fail,
bad loans and rip offs, was their Holy Grail.
The rich get richer and the poor die poor . . .
Tell me, do I need another metaphor?

The time has come, for the old and young to put down their
    guns,
and let love—give love—share love.
The time has come, on the 3rd Rock from the Sun . . .

Call of Duty

It doesn't matter who you are, or if you're rich or poor.
Thank the men and women of service,
we're who they're fighting for.

Life is not a fairy tale, go wake up Sleeping Beauty.
It's time to honor those who answered,
the Call of Duty!

So many died to keep us safe, from firemen to police.
Thank the men and women of service,
and may they rest in peace.

All we do in society, is worship cash and booty.
It's time to honor those who answered,
the Call of Duty!

A Terrorist Is Born

They've got my dad locked up in Guantanamo Bay.
And mom insists he's innocent, so damn the U.S.A.

She says they come over here, because the oil makes dollars.
Start unnecessary wars, and don't believe in Allah.

Last week her best friend, was killed in a drone strike.
They call it collateral damage, because The Price is Right.

Some lives seem to matter, much more than others.
Like when your Savior is born of a Virgin Mother.

It's the tornadoes of hate, that keep the world turning.
Has everyone forgotten about Donald Sterling?

This cycle of death, can't help but go on and on . . .
We've been doing this ever since Babylon!

ANY IS TOO MANY!

I watch a white truck run over a hundred innocent humans.
Now I just don't want to see another cloud mushroomin'.

I can't feel a Pulse and I'm on vacation in Orlando.
Because one nut decides to go all commando?

Revenge was the motive in the Lone Star State.
Yet the only outcome is more heartache.

You go to the airport and the luggage goes boom!
Someone just got forty virgins in his padded tomb.

The earth is brimming with hate, and it's spreading like cancer.
Is religion the virus, or is it the answer?

As the world returns to the Dark Ages . . .
As death and destruction rampages.

When it comes to taking another innocent life . . .
ANY IS TOO MANY for my appetite!

Just Love Everybody

With all of the disputes, and problems in the world.
You've got to respect every man, woman, boy, and girl.
As long as I never-ever, hurt anyone else.
Then everyone should just worry about themselves.

You might disagree with the style of my hair,
the clothes that I wear,
or the tattoos I bare—it's true.
But just let me be me, and I'll let you be you.

Treat me like I wanna be treated,
need me like I need to be needed,
and greet me like I wanna be greeted.
Open up your heart . . .

It doesn't matter who you are,
we're all the same in the graveyard.
It doesn't matter where you're from,
we'll only survive if the old and young . . .

Just Love Everybody—all around the world—love
    everybody . . .

My Time to Shine!

I may not be another Einstein,
but this soliloquy of syntax is my design.

Some things happen only once in a lifetime.
When mere words can shift the paradigm.

So put my name in lights,
up on the Hollywood sign.
Book me as guest for a week,
on What's My Line.

From Columbine to Palestine,
keep looking for the mastermind.
Because poetry's been redefined,
and it's my time to shine!

Poetic Therapy

When I want a drink,
I go down Bourbon Street.
So tipsy I lip-sync,
and sound like R & B.

They call me Humperdinck,
because I love to breed.
You'll find the missing link,
hiding above my knees.

This ship will never sink,
it's puffing on seaweed.
Before my forty winks,
a shot of Hennessy.

When I have to think,
I turn off the TV.
But if I need a shrink . . .
Poetic Therapy!

Acknowledgments

This book is dedicated to my dear mother, Norma Burks, who wove the gift of creativity into the fabric of my soul. And to my siblings Dee, Jeff, Tracey, and my identical twin, Marc.

I hope this is something my children can be proud of: Kailyn, Jasmine, Alexis, Kyle, and Brittany. To Sondra: *We have a rare chemistry, just enough to last for eternity.*

I appreciate my second family of Alison, Carol, Janice, Mary, Sandy, Kristin, Christy, and Lene, who usually get to read it first. *The world's a lonely place, it's an open and shut case.* Thanks for the memories, whether ahead of us or behind.

My brothers from another mother: Steve, Shabaka, Rudy, Bill, Tom, Clarence, Jon, Don, Frank, Mark, and Randy. *The ties that bind, will never unwind.*

I thank everyone else who allows me to grace their presence in the spirit of friendship.

Meet the Author

Greg Ware has been an educator/administrator in California's San Gabriel Valley for the last fifteen years. He has a Master's Degree in Education and a teaching credential from Nova Southeastern University in Florida. In addition to nurturing young minds, Greg is an accomplished musician and producer with a Billboard Top-Forty hit to his credit, along with over twenty songs featured on television. His ability to pen humorous and quirky songs opened the door to writing comedy. Greg honed his craft under the tutelage of comedian Bobbie Oliver at the legendary Ice House in Pasadena, California. After a memorable performance there he was invited to take his routine to the Main Room at the iconic Comedy Store in Hollywood! Yet writing lyrics and jokes only satisfied a fraction of his evolving fascination with the divine purpose of humanity.

These poems are designed to enlighten and entertain, as there's more than one way to peel a parable. Yet the fruits of knowledge ripen in the highest branches, rarely harvested . . . Greg is also the best-selling author of the sci-fi inspirational thriller entitled "Just Love Everybody." This is an interactive novel with an accompanying CD of the same title, as the author showcases his musicality.

Greg is currently writing his next novel. He can be contacted at GregWare@twinapath . . . Justloveeverybody1@gmail.com . . . Justloveeverybody.com.